# QUICK DIVE

# INTO

# WEB API

The goal of this book is to provide a quick overview of Web API. This book covers fundamentals of Web API and introduces you to some complex topics like tokenization, setting up API to accept only HTTPS, API Versioning, and CORS. We will also learn how to test WEB API. I strongly recommend readers of this book to practice along and get some hands-on experience.

Why you should buy this book:

a) For a quick overview of Web API.
b) Free Support: You can email me at cloudsimplifiedforyou@gmail.com for any questions (technical or related to book) you may have. Typically, I will answer your question in 1-2 business days. Please limit your questions to topics discussed in this book. Thank you, kindly.

# Table of Contents

The goal of this chapter is to introduce you to asynchronous programming. The concepts that we learn in the chapter will help us to design an efficient WEB API.

As developers, we are always challenged with the task of making applications more responsive. One way to achieve this is by using Asynchronous programming. Traditional ways of writing asynchronous applications are complicated, difficult to write and maintain. To overcome these challenges, Microsoft introduced the concept of "Async" and "Await".

Let us take a step backward and talk about synchronous programming. In synchronous programming, we call a method and wait for the results to come back. The calling program, which may be a UI or a service, will be non-responsive until results are back. In cases where we want to do some expensive calculations or some I/O operations, we do not want our application to hang and wait for the results.

**Example**: Let us say we have created a new windows application and added a Form with a button and a grid. When user clicks on this button, we want to call a method that will do some complex calculations. It can take up to 20 seconds to complete. We want to display results of this method on the grid. If we do synchronous programming then for these 20 seconds, user cannot do anything on the form. They cannot minimize the form or do any kind of operation. Ideally, what we would like is, UI should stay responsive during these 20 seconds. User should be able to interact with the form. Let us see how we can achieve this using Async and Await.

"async" keyword enables the "await" keyword. That's all it does. Await is where all the magic happens. What "await" does is, it takes a single argument (an awaitable). Await examines that awaitable and checks if it has completed. If completed, method runs like a synchronous process. Otherwise, it returns from the async method and tells awaitable to run when method has completed. Method marked as "async" must return one of these: Task, Task<T> or void. At first, all this sounds very complicated, but let us look at an example and understand it.

Exercise: Create an application that uses Aysnc and Await

In this exercise, we are going to create a new windows based application, add a "Button" and a "Text box" on the Form. On click of the button, we are going to call a method "DoComplexCalculations". Inside this method, we are going to call another method "Concatenate" using "Task.Run". We are going to use await while calling this method. What await will do is, as soon as we queue the work that we will do in "concatenate" method; it will return control back to the calling program. Because it gives the control back, calling program should continue running next statements until it sees "Await" statement. So, right after calling this method, we will assign textbox a value of "1". Our next statement after assigning textbox, a value of "1 will be an await statement (await jsonTask). What that is going to do is, it will wait for the results to come back from "DoComplexCalculations" method. The control will be passed back to UI and hence UI should become responsive and stay like that during the time work is done in "Concatenate" method. User should be able to minimize the form or even close it. After the await statement, we are going to assign a textbox a value of "2".

Let us get started with our application:

1. Create a new Windows Application.
2. Add one Button on the form. Go to the properties of button and name it as "btnAsyncOperation".
3. Then add one Textbox on the form. Name it: "txtResults"
4. On the click event of the button, add the following code:

```csharp
private async void btnAsyncOperation_Click(object sender, EventArgs e)
{
    var jsonTask = Async.DoComplexCalculations();
    txtResults.Text = "1";

    await jsonTask;
    txtResults.Text = "2";
}
```

5. Add a new class to the project. Name it "Async".
6. Copy the following code in the class

```csharp
using System.Text;
using System.Threading.Tasks;

namespace test
{
 public class Async
 {
        public static async Task<string> DoComplexCalculations()
        {
           var jsonString = await Task.Run(() => Concatenate());

           return jsonString;
        }

    private static string Concatenate()
        {

          StringBuilder jsonString1 = new StringBuilder();

           for (int count = 0; count < 10000000; count ++)
             {
               jsonString1 = jsonString1.Append(count + "b");
             }

          return jsonString1.ToString();
        }

  }
 }
```

7. Run the project to see how Async/Await can make UI responsive.

Expected Behavior of the application:

1) Initially Text Box should get value of "1".
2) Form should remain responsive and you should be able to minimize the form.
3) After all the work is finished in "DoComplexCalculations" method, Text Box should get value of "2".

## What we are going to build:

We are going to build an API that can maintain list of Certificates and Users. Through this API, organizations can add Certifications. Let us say, company ABC gives .NET certification. User "A" enrolls into the program and completes .NET certification. Through this API, company ABC can add certification (Database Table: "Certifications"), can add User A (Database Table: Users), and once User A completes certification, he/she should be able to see all his/her certifications (stored in Database Table: "UsersCertifications"). Let us assume a third-party program will populate data in table "UsersCertifications". We will also talk about how we can implement tokenization to make our API secure. In the end, I will show you how we can achieve versioning in API.

We are going to use/learn SQL 2014, EF 6.0, Repository pattern, Routing attributes, AuthorizationFilterAttribute, CORS, Ninject for Dependency Injection, Basic Authentication and Tokenization.

In this chapter, we will start building our first API. I am going to use Visual Studio 2015.

1) Open Visual Studio and click on File-> New-> Project.

2) Select "ASP.NET Web Application" under Web and click on "Ok" button. Enter name as "WebAPI". If you already have a project name "WebAPI" on your computer, you can enter a different name or choose a different location.

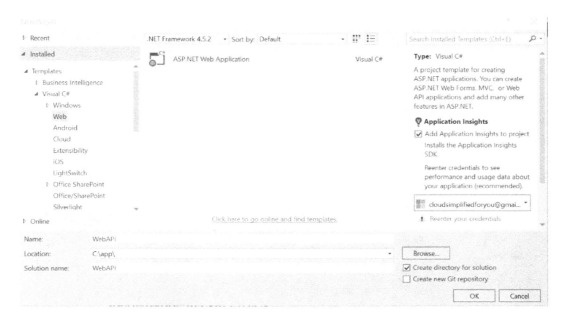

3) Then select "Web API" and click on "Ok" button.

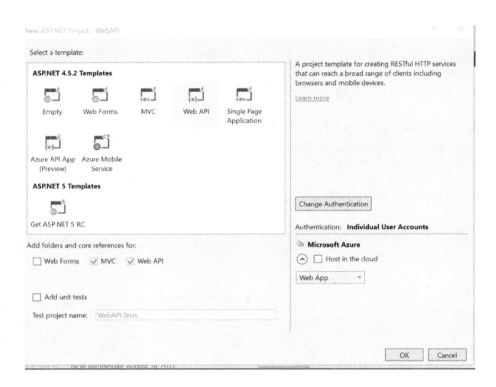

4) For our exercise, API will read data from SQL Server. We are going to create a class library that will use EF 6.0 to access data from SQL Server. So, let us add this class library project and name it as "Data Access".

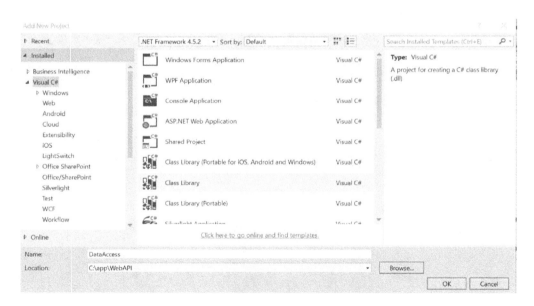

5) Next, we will add NuGet package for Entity Framework. Go to Tools->NuGet Package Manager->Manage NuGet Packages for Solution.

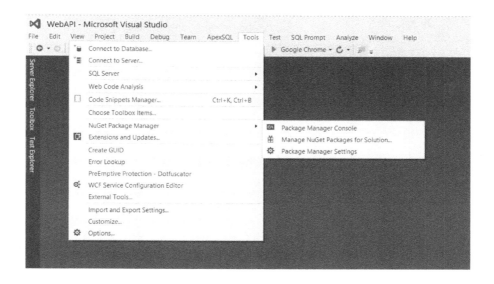

6) Search for Entity Framework and add it to solution.

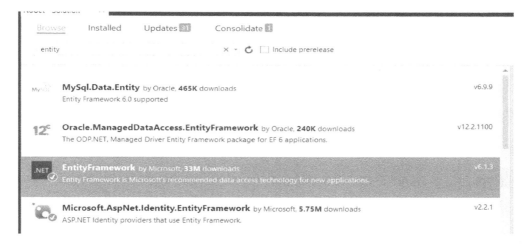

7) Install 6.1.3 version. If you see any latest version, feel free to install that.

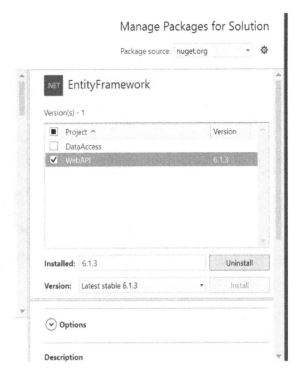

8) Open SQL Management Studio. If you have SQL Server installed on your local machine, you can connect to it. If not, then you can download SQL Server 2014 Express from Microsoft Website. We are going to create a new database in SQL Server. Right click databases, select "New Database", and name it "Certifications". Then to create database tables, please run the following three SQL scripts in your database.

You can download these scripts from the following link:

https://github.com/auppal80/WEB-API-Demo/tree/master/Database

Run them in following order:

1) DatabaseScripts.sql

2) DatabaseScripts1.sql

3) DatabaseScripts2.sql

4) Next step is to add a user to the database. If you do not want to change "Web.Config" then add a user with name "Test" and password "test" to database. Make sure this user belongs to "sysadmin" Role. However if you would like, you can create a different user and change web.config accordingly.

# Chapter Three – Create EDMX

In this chapter, we are going to add EDMX and create repository. We created a class library for our data access in the previous chapter. Now, we will add Entity Data Model to this library.

1. To do so, click on "Add New Item" and select "ADO.NET Entity Data Model". In the Name Text box, type "Certification". Then click on "Add" button.

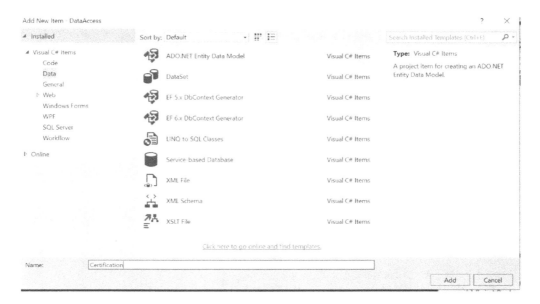

2. After you click on "Add" button, you will be asked to select how you want to build your entity data model. For this exercise, select "EF Designer from Database".

Entity Data Model Wizard     ✕

**Choose Model Contents**

**What should the model contain?**

EF Designer from database    Empty EF Designer model    Empty Code First model    Code First from database

Creates a model in the EF Designer based on an existing database. You can choose the database connection, settings for the model, and database objects to include in the model. The classes your application will interact with are generated from the model.

< Previous    Next >    Finish    Cancel

3) Click on the "Next" button.

4) You will be presented with the following screen. Choose your SQL Server name, database name and click on "Ok" button.

5) It will create EDMX, run T4 templates that will create models and Context class from EDMX.

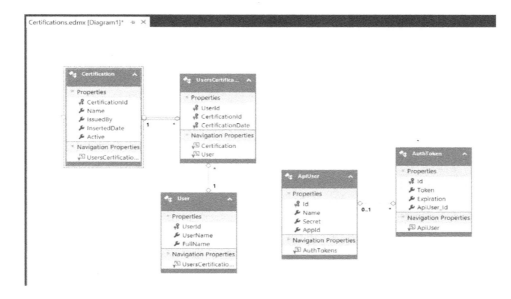

Let us look at the files that are generated after we create EDMX. Under your EDMX file, you will see a file named "Certifications.tt" (see snapshot below). This is a T4 template. This template will read from EDMX and create models(entities) for us. If you want to run this template manually, you can do so by right clicking on "Certifications.tt" file and then by clicking on "Run Custom Tool".

"Certifications.Context.tt" is another T4 template. Running this template creates DbContext class (see "Certifications.Context.cs" file). This class is a bridge between entity classes and database. It allows us to establish connection to database and query from database tables.

# Chapter Four – Repository Pattern

In the previous chapter, we created entities from database. In this chapter, we are going to use repository pattern to access data from database. There are number of ways to implement repository pattern. Most common being to use unit of work and repository pattern. However, for our exercise, we are going to keep it simple.

Add a new Class to "DataAccess" Project. Name this class as "CertificationsRepository". Also, add a new interface class "ICertificationRespository.cs" to the project. "CertificationsRepository" class is going to implement interface "ICertificationRespository.cs". By doing so, we will make our code easy to test and as we will see later, it will help us to do dependency injection. We are going to add all methods that read or write to database in this class.

The way repository pattern works is, it is going to use DbContext class "CertificationsEntities" to query data from database.

If you would like to download project and look at code, please go to the link below.

https://github.com/auppal80/WEB-API-Demo/tree/master/WebAPI

## Exercise: Building the Repository Class

In this exercise, we are going to build the repository class. As mentioned earlier, repository class will use DbContext class. Therefore, constructor of repository class will accept instance of DbContext class a parameter. In chapter 6, we will learn how to use Ninject to inject instance of DbContext class into repository.

### Constructor for Repository Class:

```csharp
public class CertificationsRepository : ICertificationRespository
    {
        private CertificationsEntities _ctx;

        public CertificationsRepository(CertificationsEntities ctx)
        {
            _ctx = ctx;
        }
```

Note: CertificationsEntities inherits from DbContext class.

### Getting Data using LINQ:

In general, to get data from Table "SampleTable" for field "SampleTableId" with a value of "Id" we can say DbContextClass.SampleTable.Where(st=>st. SampleTableId == Id).FirstOrDefault();

Therefore, in our case, if we want to get a Certification from "Certifications" table, where field "CertificationId" has a value of "1" we can say ctx.Certifications.Where(c=>c.CertificationId =1).FirstOrDefault(). Here "ctx" is an instance of "CertificationsEntities". As you can see in the code below, this is what "GetCertificationByCertificatId" method is doing. It accepts "Id" as input parameter and returns Entity of Type Certification that has "CertificationId" value equal to input parameter.

Now for our next method, let us assume following

1) We have lot of certifications in our database and our requirement is to return all certifications,
   when a client makes a "Get" request without any input parameters.
2) It takes about 5 seconds to fetch all certifications from database.

In chapter 1, we learned about asynchronous programming. We are going to make use of that now. We want to make sure that client can do other operations, while we fetch all certifications from database. Therefore, our "GetAllCertifications" method will return a Task of List<Certifications>. See code below.

*Code to get All Certifications from Database :*

```
public Task<List<Certification>> GetAllCertifications()
    {
        return Task.Run(() => _ctx.Certifications.Where(c => c.Active ==
                                            true).ToList()
                                            );

    }


public Certification GetCertificationbyCertificationId(int Id)
    {
            return _ctx.Certifications.Where(c => c.CertificationId ==
                                            Id).FirstOrDefault();
    }
```

Similarly, we can write more methods to get data from other tables, based on different parameters.


## Adding and Deleting Data:

Now, we are going to write methods to add or delete Certifications from database.

To add a certification, we can say _ctx.Certifications.Add(Entity). Here "_ctx" is instance of class that inherits from DbContext, Certifications is of type "DbSet" and Entity is our instance of Certification that we want to add.

When we want to delete a certification, we should first check and make sure that certification exists in the database. If it does, then we delete it. Look at "DeleteCertification" method below, this is exactly what it is doing.

*Code to Add or Delete Certifications from Database:*

```
public bool InsertCertification(Certification entry)
    {
        try
        {
            _ctx.Certifications.Add(entry);
            return true;
        }
        catch
        {
            return false;
        }
    }


public bool DeleteCertification(int id)
    {
        try
        {
            var entity = _ctx.Certifications.Where(d => d.CertificationId ==
                    id).FirstOrDefault();
            if (entity != null)
            {
                _ctx.Certifications.Remove(entity);
                return true;
            }
        }
        catch
        {//log error
        }

        return false;
    }


public bool SaveAll()
    {
        return _ctx.SaveChanges() > 0;
    }
```

Similarly, we can write methods to delete or add to other tables. You can look at some other methods in my project on GitHub.

## Calling Repository code from Controller:

Now that we have written code for repository, let us see how we can call this code from controller. Remember we have not created any controller yet. In the chapter on controller, we will learn more about writing code for controller. I just quickly wanted to show, how to call repository code from controller. If you are not familiar with MVC pattern, you can skip this section and go to Chapter 5. We are going to call "DeleteCertification" method from controller.

When a delete request come, routing controller will use registered routes to determine which controller to select and then will call "Delete" method on this selected controller. Inside this delete method, we should first check and make sure that "Certification" that user is trying to delete exists. This can be achieved by calling "GetCertificationbyCertificationId" method on the Repository. If it exists, we can remove it by calling "DeleteCertification" method on repository and then by calling "SaveAll" method to commit all changes to database. If it does not exist, then we can return Error 400(Bad Request) to the client.

*Controller Code to call Delete Method on Repository:*

```
[Route("{id:int}")]
public IHttpActionResult Delete(int id)
 {
    var entity = TheRepository.GetCertificationbyCertificationId(id);
    if (entity == null)
     {
      return NotFound();
     }

    if (TheRepository.DeleteCertification(entity.CertificationId) &&
       TheRepository.SaveAll())
     {
      return Ok();
     }
    return BadRequest();
 }
```

Routing is how WEB API matches an incoming request to an action. Actions are public methods on the controller. Web API routing is similar to ASP.NET MVC routing. We can do convention-based or attribute based routing. In convention-based routing, routes are defined in the Register method of the "WebApiConfig" class. This means all the routes are in one class.

Example of Convention based Route:

```
config.Routes.MapHttpRoute(
    name: "Users",
    routeTemplate: "api/users/{id}",
    defaults: new { controller = "Users", id = RouteParameter.Optional }
);
```

When the Web API framework receives a HTTP request, it tries to match the URI against one of the route templates in the routing table. For example. The following request will match above URI

a)  /api/users
b)  /api/users/1

Once a matching route is found, routing engine determines the controller and the action. Controller name is straightforward to get. It is already there in the routing table (example: **controller will be** "Users" **in the above example**) Finding the action requires some digging. Web API will look at the HTTP method, and then it will look for an action whose name begins with that HTTP method name. For example, with a GET request, Web API looks for an action that starts with "Get".

Though convention based routing is easy to understand and implement, it may not be flexible enough, depending on requirements. WEB API 2.0 introduced the concept of routing attributes. As the name suggests, it uses attributes to define routes. The advantage of using attributes based routing is that it gives us more control over the URIs.

If you open WebApiConfig.cs file (under App_Start folder), you can see that convention based routes are registered in the register method.

*Code from WebApiConfig.cs file:*

```
public static class WebApiConfig
    {
        public static void Register(HttpConfiguration config)
        {
            config.SuppressDefaultHostAuthentication();
            config.Filters.Add(new
            HostAuthenticationFilter(OAuthDefaults.AuthenticationType));
            // Web API routes
            config.MapHttpAttributeRoutes();
            config.Routes.MapHttpRoute(
```

```
            name: "Users",
            routeTemplate: "api/users/{id}",
            defaults: new { controller = "Users", id = RouteParameter.Optional }
        );
          config.Routes.MapHttpRoute(
            name: "CertifiedUsers",
            routeTemplate: "api/CertifiedUsers/{id}",
            defaults: new { controller = "CertifiedUsers" }
        );
          config.Routes.MapHttpRoute(
            name: "DefaultApi",
            routeTemplate: "api/{controller}/{id}",
            defaults: new { id = RouteParameter.Optional }
        );
          config.EnableCors();
          // config.Filters.Add(new RequiredHttpsAttribute());
      }
    }
```

Let us try to understand this code:

"Config.MapHttpAttributeRoutes" enables attribute routing. It will map the attributes defined in the application. We will look at them shortly.

The next line has routes for convention based routing:

```
config.Routes.MapHttpRoute(
        name: "Users",
        routeTemplate: "api/users/{id}",
        defaults: new { controller = "Users", id = RouteParameter.Optional }

    );
```

What it is telling is whenever the request URL has template as "api/users/{id}", select "Users" as controller. The Id parameter is optional.

## Attribute Routing

As mentioned earlier, web API 2.0 introduced the concept of Attribute Routing. What it means is we can define routes at the method or the controller level. This way we can have more control over the URIs in our API. To achieve this, we can use "RoutePrefix" attribute at the controller level or "Route" at the method level.

## Example of Route Prefix

As you can see in the snapshot below, I have put RoutePrefix("api/Certificates") at the controller level. By putting it here, I do not need to add this prefix at each method level. This route prefix will apply to all the methods in the controller. This way we can put common URL prefix for all the methods at the controller level. To customize the route at each method level, we can use Route Attribute at the method level. Either we can override prefix setting or we can add to the URL prefix.

For example: In the "Get(int id)" method, I added a Route Attribute "Route("{id}",Name ="Certificate"). What it means is that, a GET request with a URL like "api/Certificates/id" (RoutePrefix/Id) will call this method. In addition, we are giving this route a name of "Certificate".

Note: To override prefix settings at method level we can use tilde( ~).

```csharp
namespace WebAPI.Controllers
{
    [RoutePrefix("api/Certificates")]
    1 reference | auppal80, 158 days ago | 1 author, 3 changes
    public class CertificatesController : BaseApiController
    {
        const int PAGE_SIZE = 50;
        0 references | auppal80, 163 days ago | 1 author, 1 change
        public CertificatesController(ICertificationRespository repo, IGetCurrentUserIdentity getCurrentUserIdentityService) : base(repo)
        {
        }
        [Route("", Name = "Certificates")]
        0 references | auppal80, 158 days ago | 1 author, 2 changes
        public async Task<IHttpActionResult> Get(int page = 0, int page_Size = PAGE_SIZE)...
        [Route("{id}", Name = "Certificate")]
        0 references | auppal80, 161 days ago | 1 author, 2 changes
        public IHttpActionResult Get(int id)...
        [Route("")]
        0 references | auppal80, 158 days ago | 1 author, 2 changes
        public IHttpActionResult Post([FromBody] CertificateUriModel model)...


        [Route("")]
        0 references | auppal80, 158 days ago | 1 author, 1 change
        public IHttpActionResult Put([FromBody] CertificateUriModel model)...
        [Route("{id:int}")]
        0 references | auppal80, 158 days ago | 1 author, 3 changes
        public IHttpActionResult Delete(int id)...
    }
}
```

As we discussed earlier, controller uses repository pattern to query data from database. To maintain separation of concerns we do not want controller to be responsible for creation of repository or any of its dependencies. Remember from the previous chapter that, repository is dependent on DbContext class. If we let controller instantiate repository class then it will have to first create instance of "CertificationsEntities". This will make our system tightly coupled. Therefore, to get around this, we are going to use "Ninject". We will inject Repository into every controller using Ninject and BaseApiController.

To use Ninject first we need to add two NuGet packages

1)  Add NuGet package "Ninject.Mvc3" to the project.  Ghg

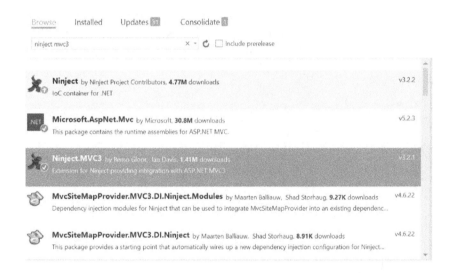

When you add this, it will add "NinjectWebCommon" class under the "App_start" folder.

Here is a snapshot of "NinjectWebCommon" class.

```
NinjectWebCommon.cs  ⊡ ✕
WebAPI                                          ▼  ⚙WebAPI.App_Start.NinjectWebCommon
 5   ⊟namespace WebAPI.App_Start
 6    {
 7   ⊞    using ...
          2 references | auppe80  13 days ago | 1 author 1 change
16   ⊟    public static class NinjectWebCommon
17    {
18            private static readonly Bootstrapper bootstrapper = new Bootstrapper();
19
20   ⊞        /// <summary> Starts the application
              0 references | auppe80  14 days ago | 1 author 1 change
23   ⊞        public static void Start() ...
29
30   ⊞        /// <summary> Stops the application.
              0 references | auppe80  14 days ago | 1 author 1 change
33   ⊞        public static void Stop()...
37
38   ⊞        /// <summary> Creates the kernel that will manage your application.
              1 reference | auppe80  12 days ago | 1 author 2 changes
42   ⊞        private static IKernel CreateKernel()...
62
63   ⊞        /// <summary> Load your modules or register your services here!
              1 reference | auppe80  12 days ago | 1 author 2 changes
67   ⊞        private static void RegisterServices(IKernel kernel)...
73    }
74    }
75
```

2) Then add NuGet package "WebApiContrib.IoC.Ninject" to the project.
3) After you add these NuGet packages, add the following in the "CreateKernel" method of file "NinjectWebCommon" class.

```
private static IKernel CreateKernel()
{
    var kernel = new StandardKernel();
    try
    {
      kernel.Bind<Func<IKernel>>().ToMethod(ctx => () => new
      Bootstrapper().Kernel);

      kernel.Bind<IHttpModule>().To<HttpApplicationInitializationHttpModul
      e>();

        GlobalConfiguration.Configuration.DependencyResolver =
        new NinjectResolver(kernel);

        RegisterServices(kernel);

        return kernel;
    }
    catch
    {
        kernel.Dispose();
        throw;
    }
}
```

4) Then add the following code in the "RegisterServices" Method in the "NinjectWebCommon" class. This code will register the Repository and Context class with Ninject.

```
    Private static void RegisterServices(IKernel kernel)
    {

     kernel.Bind<ICertificationRespository>().To<CertificationsRepository>();
```

25

```
kernel.Bind<CertificationsEntities>().To<CertificationsEntities>();
kernel.Bind<IGetCurrentUserIdentity>().To<GetCurrentUserIdentity>();
}
```

We have not talked about "GetCurrentUserIdentity" class yet. The role of this class is to get the Identity of the current user. Create a "services" folder under your project and add interface and class for identity class to your project.

*Code for Identity Class:*

```
public interface IGetCurrentUserIdentity
    {
        string CurrentUser { get; }
    }


public class GetCurrentUserIdentity: IGetCurrentUserIdentity
    {
        public string CurrentUser
        {
            get
            { return Thread.CurrentPrincipal.Identity.Name; }

        }
    }
```

Now that we have created repository class and registered it, we can start creating controllers. We will first create a Base Controller class. All controllers will inherit from this class. The idea behind creating base class is that we will inject repository into the base controller. Thus, all controllers that inherit from base controller will have access to repository.

We will also create a model factory class. This class will be responsible for transforming models that we get from database into models that we want to return to client. This could involve adding, modifying or removing some properties to the model that we get from the database. For example, we will add a URI property, which will have link for current page in every model, serialize it and return to client.

Example: As you can see "Create" method below takes model of type "Certification" and returns model of Type "CertificateUriModel".

*Sample Code for Model Factory:*

```
public class ModelFactory
    {
        private UrlHelper _urlHelper;

        public ModelFactory(HttpRequestMessage request)
        {
            _urlHelper = new UrlHelper(request);

        }

        public CertificateUriModel Create(Certification oc)
        {
            return new CertificateUriModel()
            {
                CertificationId = oc.CertificationId,
                Name = oc.Name,
                Active = oc.Active,
                InsertedDate = oc.InsertedDate,
                IssuedBy = oc.IssuedBy,
                Url = _urlHelper.Link("Certificate", new { id = oc.CertificationId })
            };
        }

}
```

We are not going to inject Model factory into controllers. To create URl for current page or next page, Model factory will create an instance of UrlHelper.UrlHelper constructor accepts "HttpRequestMessage". Since "HttpRequestMessage" is available only when a request is made so we will create instance of Model Factory in the method, instead of injecting it.

Here is how CertificateUriModel model looks like. It has some properties from the Certification Model and a "Url" property to store link for current page.

```
public class CertificateUriModel
{
    public int CertificationId { get; set; }
    public string Name { get; set; }
    public string IssuedBy { get; set; }
    public System.DateTime InsertedDate { get; set; }
    public bool Active { get; set; }
    public string Url { get; set; }
}
```

Now back to the code for Base Controller. We have already registered Repository with Ninject. As you can see below, we are injecting Repository into the base API Controller. All controllers can use Repository Property on the base controller to get access of repository.

*Code for Base Controller:*

```
Public abstract class BaseApiController: ApiController
{
    ICertificationRespository _repo;

    ModelFactory _modelFactory;
    public BaseApiController(ICertificationRespository repo)
    {
        _repo = repo;
    }

    protected ICertificationRespository TheRepository
    {
        get
        {
            return _repo;
        }
    }
    protected ModelFactory TheModelFactory
    {
        get
        {
            if (_modelFactory == null)
            {
                _modelFactory = new ModelFactory(this.Request);
            }
            return _modelFactory;
        }
    }
}
```

Now add a new class called "CertificatesController" to the controllers folder. This class will inherit from BaseApiController class. We will implement Get, Post, Put and Delete method in it.

For Get method, we will write two methods. One will get all certificates from database, order them by name and convert them to List of CertificateUriModel using Model Factory. Other method will take "Id" as input parameter, get Certification for this "Id" from database and convert it to CertificateUriModel.

For Post, Client will put CertificateUriModel in the body. We will read this CertificateUriModel, check and make sure that a certificate with same name does not exist in database. If it exists, we will return 409 error (Conflict). If it does not, we will convert this CertificateUriModel to database model and save it in database by calling the Save method on the repository. If Save is successful, we will return status code 201 (Created).

For Delete, Client will pass Id of certificate to be deleted in the URL. First, we will check and make sure Certificate with that ID exists in database. If it does not, controller will call NotFound() method to return 404(Not Found) response.

*Code for Certificates Controller:*

```
[RoutePrefix("api/Certificates")]
public class CertificatesController : BaseApiController
{
  const int PAGE_SIZE = 50;

    public CertificatesController(ICertificationRespository repo,  IGetCurrentUserIdentity
    getCurrentUserIdentityService) : base(repo)
  {
  }

  [Route("", Name = "Certificates")]
  public async Task<IHttpActionResult> Get()
  {
    var certifications = TheRepository.GetAllCertifications();
    // we can do some calculations or some work here if we need to.
    await certifications;

    var orderedCertifications = certifications.Result.OrderBy(c => c.Name);

        return Ok(orderedCertifications.Select(oc =>
            TheModelFactory.Create(oc)).ToList(););
  }


  [Route("{id}", Name = "Certificate")]
    public IHttpActionResult Get(int id)
    {
      var certfication = TheRepository.GetCertificationbyCertificationId(id);
```

```
        if (certfication == null)
        {
            return NotFound();
        }
        else
        {
            return Ok(TheModelFactory.Create(certfication));
        }
    }

    [Route("")]
public IHttpActionResult Post([FromBody] CertificateUriModel model)
{
    if (TheRepository.GetCertificationByName(model.Name) != null)
    {  // 409 error
        return Conflict();
    }

    var modelCertificate = TheModelFactory.Convert(model);

    if (TheRepository.InsertCertification(modelCertificate) &&
        TheRepository.SaveAll())
    {
        var modelUriCreated= TheModelFactory.Create(modelCertificate);
        return Created(modelUriCreated.Url, modelUriCreated);
    }

    return BadRequest();
}

[Route("")]
public IHttpActionResult Put([FromBody] CertificateUriModel model)
{
    if (TheRepository.GetCertificationByName(model.Name) != null)
    {
        return Conflict();
    }

    if (TheRepository.UpdateCertification(TheModelFactory.Convert(model)) &&
        TheRepository.SaveAll())
    {
     return
     Created(TheModelFactory.Create(TheModelFactory.Convert(model)).Url, model);
    }

    return BadRequest();
}
```

```csharp
[Route("{id:int}")]
public IHttpActionResult Delete(int id)
{
    var entity = TheRepository.GetCertificationbyCertificationId(id);

    if (entity == null)
    {
        return NotFound();
    }

    if (TheRepository.DeleteCertification(entity.CertificationId) &&
        TheRepository.SaveAll())
    {
        return Ok();
    }

    return BadRequest();
}
```

We will use Fiddler to test Web API. If you do not have fiddler installed on your computer, please download it.

After you have written all methods for your API, you can right click the solution and publish it to a local folder on your computer. For this exercise, I published code on "C:\publish" folder. Then go into IIS and set up a new application. For our exercise, I am using port 8081. Before starting testing, open SQL management studio and put some dummy data into your tables.

Once your site is up and running, open fiddler, go to the "Composer" tab, and select "Get". Type in the URL "http://localhost:8081/api/Certificates" and click on "Execute" button. If everything works correctly, we should get all certificates from the database.

When we click on "Execute" button, it makes a "Get" request. Since we did not specify "Accept" in the request header, so we will get JSON object back by default. As expected and seen below we got all the certificates from database.

Now we will make another "Get" request but this time we want to get Certificate that has Id of "3". Our URL will be "http://localhost:8081/api/certificates/3".

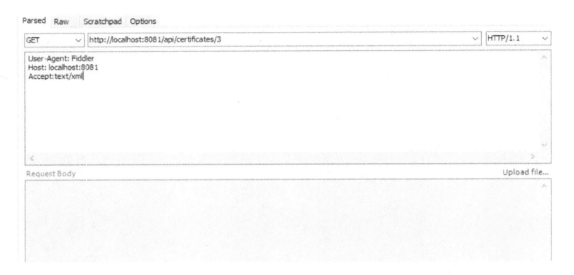

As you can see above that in the Request header, I have specifically mentioned that we accept XML as return type. After we click on "Execute" button, we get response as shown below.

Let us now do a Post operation and insert a new entry into database. Choose method as "POST" and put data as shown below in the request body. Then click on "Execute" button.

If everything works successfully, we should get 201(Created) response code back. It means that request has been completed and resource has been created.

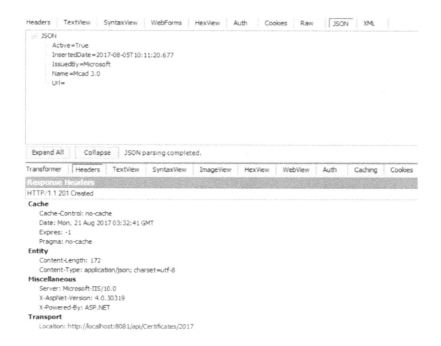

Let us now test delete. Select "DELETE" as a method. We are going to delete resource with id: 1003. Therefore, our URL will be "http://localhost:8081/api/certificates/1003". Click on Execute button and if there are no foreign key constraints error, Certificate with Id of 1003 should get deleted from database.

Response:

DELETE /api/certificates/2005 HTTP/1.1
**Client**
    User-Agent: Fiddler
**Entity**
    Content-Length: 0
    content-type: application/json
**Transport**
    Host: localhost:8081

| Transformer | Headers | TextView | SyntaxView | ImageView | HexView | WebView |
|---|---|---|---|---|---|---|

**Response Headers**

HTTP/1.1 200 OK
**Cache**
    Cache-Control: no-cache
    Date: Mon, 21 Aug 2017 03:34:54 GMT
    Expires: -1
    Pragma: no-cache
**Entity**
    Content-Length: 0
**Miscellaneous**
    Server: Microsoft-IIS/10.0
    X-AspNet-Version: 4.0.30319
    X-Powered-By: ASP.NET

Our API should support pagination. Instead of sending thousands of records together to the client, we should send only few records at a time, and only if clients request for more records, we should send them more. This means that we should keep track of how many records we have already send, and we should have the ability to figure out next set of records.

Let us take an example: We have 500 certificates in our database. Client has a UI page with a grid that displays only 100 records at a time. It means we just need to fetch first 100 records initially and display. Hence, our page size is 100. Total number of pages will be 500/100(number of records/page size) =5.

When client makes a request for all certificates, along with request they should send us page size and page number. They can pass this information in the query string. Initially page number is "0", so we go to database and get first 100 records. After that when client needs more records, they send us another request, with page number as "1" and page size as "100". When we receive this request, we will go to database again, ignore first 100 records and get next set of 100 records. In our response back to the client, we should also give them, a link to next and previous page. This will help them in navigation.

To create links for next page and previous page, we can use "UrlHelper" and pass Request to it.

We will modify the Get method that we created earlier to achieve following:

a) Asynchronously Call "GetAllCertifications" method on repository.
b) Wait for the results to come back. If needed, we can do some work between the time we call method and get results.
c) Next, we determine number of records returned. The, we divide it by page size to get number of pages.
d) Then we create an instance of UrlHelper. We can use "Link" method on UrlHelper to create URL for next and previous page.
e) Our goal is to populate CertificatePageModel, which consists of nextPage, prevPage and List<CertificateUriModel>.

*Code for Implementing Paging:*

```
public async Task<IHttpActionResult> Get(int page = 0, int page_Size = PAGE_SIZE)
    {
            var certifications = TheRepository.GetAllCertifications();
            // we can do some calculations or some work here if we need to.
            await certifications;

            var orderedCertifications = certifications.Result.OrderBy(c => c.Name);
            var totalCount = orderedCertifications.Count();
            var totalPages = Math.Ceiling((double)totalCount / page_Size);

            var helper = new UrlHelper(Request);
```

```csharp
var certificatePageModel = new CertificatePageModel();

if (page > 0)
{
    certificatePageModel.prevPage = helper.Link("Certificates", new { page =
    page - 1 });
}
else
{
    certificatePageModel.prevPage = "";
}

if (page < totalPages - 1)
{
    certificatePageModel.nextPage = helper.Link("Certificates", new { page =
    page + 1 });
}
else
{

    certificatePageModel.nextPage = "";
}

certificatePageModel.CertificateUrIModelList =
                            orderedCertifications.Skip(page_Size * page)
                            .Take(page_Size)
                            .ToList().Select(oc =>
                            TheModelFactory.Create(oc)).ToList();

return Ok(certificatePageModel);
}
```

If your API is public and anyone can use it, you do not have to worry much about authentication and authorization. However, more often, we want to limit access to our API's. We want to make sure user making the request is valid user and has permission to access resources. Let us talk about how we can control access.

## Basic Authentication:

In basic authentication, user will pass user name and password every time they make a request. Of course, password will be encrypted.

To implement this, we will create a class that will inherit from "AuthorizationFilterAttribute" and override the "OnAuthorization" method. In this method, we will check if the authorization header has been passed along with request. If it has been passed, then we will extract username and password out of it. Once we have these, we can validate them against database and make sure user is valid. If user does not exists in our database or user does not have permissions, we can return HttpStatusCode "Unauthorized".

*Code for implementing Basic Authentication:*

```
public class BasicAuthenticationAttribute : AuthorizationFilterAttribute
    {

        public override void OnAuthorization(HttpActionContext actionContext)
        {
            var authHeader = actionContext.Request.Headers.Authorization;

            if (authHeader != null)
            {
                if (authHeader.Scheme.Equals("basic", StringComparison.OrdinalIgnoreCase)
                                    &&
                            !string.IsNullOrWhiteSpace(authHeader.Parameter))
                {
                    var rawCredentials = authHeader.Parameter;
                    var encoding = Encoding.GetEncoding("iso-8859-1");
                        var credentials =
                    encoding.GetString(Convert.FromBase64String(rawCredentials));
                    var split = credentials.Split(':');
                    var username = split[0];
                    var password = split[1];

                    if (ValidateUser(username, password))
                    {
                        var principal = new GenericPrincipal(new
                                        GenericIdentity(username), null);
                        Thread.CurrentPrincipal = principal;
```

```
                return;
            }
        }
    }

    actionContext.Response =
                    actionContext.Request.CreateResponse(HttpStatusCode.Unauthorized);
}

private Boolean ValidateUser(string username, string password)
{
    // you can write code to check from database and make sure user is valid.
    return true;
}

}
```

The problem with this approach is that user will have to pass username and password with every request. What that means is, if hackers can get into the request and get username and password, they will be able to do more damage.

Tokenization:

Let us see how we can improve security-using tokenization. There are number of ways we can implement tokenization.

First, we will talk about a simple way to do it. Let us say for first request, user passes username and password. We validate the user against our "Users" table in the database. After validating user, we create a token (some GUID) and assign this token an expiration date time. We will store this token, user id for which token has been created and expiration date time in the database. Let us assume, this token is valid for next "X" number of hours. For any request that this user will make in next "X" number of hours, user does not need to send us password. They can just send us token and user Id. If "X" number of hours have passed, then the token has expired, and this user will have to send us username and password again and get a new token.

The advantage here is, even if the hackers are able to hack and get our token, they can only do damage for X number of hours. After that token will expire and their request will not be authorized.

Now let us look at another way of implementing tokenization, Let us say we ask client to register on our website. As they register, we give them API key and a Shared Key. We also store these keys in our database. When client wants to send a request to us, they will first build a string by combining API Key, HTTP method, request URI, timestamp, nonce, base 64 representation of the request. Nonce is like a unique key for the request; server can use this key to check if this is a duplicate request. Then they will hash this string using a hash algorithm and Secret Key. The result for this hash is called signature for request. The signature will be sent in the authorization header. The data in authorization header will contain API Key, Signature, Request Time stamp and nonce. Client will make a request to the token controller.

When a request is received on the server side, we will extract API Key, go to our database and get Secret key for the client. Then we will rebuild signature using shared key that we get from database. If this signature matches to the one that we got with request, we will create a Token for client and return it; otherwise, we will return 401 error.

*Code for Generating Token:*

```
public class TokenController : BaseApiController
    {
        public TokenController(ICertificationRespository repo) : base(repo)
        {

        }

        public HttpResponseMessage Post([FromBody]TokenRequestModel model)
        {
            try
            {
                var user = TheRepository.GetApiUsers().Where(u => u.AppId ==
                                        model.ApiKey).FirstOrDefault();
                if (user != null)
                {
                    var secret = user.Secret;
                    var key = Convert.FromBase64String(secret);

                    HMACSHA256 provider = new HMACSHA256(key);
                    byte[] hash = provider.ComputeHash(Encoding.UTF8.GetBytes(user.AppId));
                    string signature = Convert.ToBase64String(hash);

                    if (signature == model.Signature)
                    {
                        var rawTokenInfo = string.Concat(user.AppId + DateTime.UtcNow.ToString("d"));
                        var rawTokenByte = Encoding.UTF8.GetBytes(rawTokenInfo);
                        var token = provider.ComputeHash(rawTokenByte);
                        var authToken = new AuthToken()
                        {
                            Token = Convert.ToBase64String(token),
                            Expiration = DateTime.UtcNow.AddDays(7),
                            ApiUser = user
                        };

                        if (TheRepository.Insert(authToken) && TheRepository.SaveAll())
                        {
                            return Request.CreateResponse(HttpStatusCode.Created,
                                    TheModelFactory.Create(authToken));
```

```
              }
            }
          }
        }
      catch (Exception ex)
      {
          return Request.CreateErrorResponse(HttpStatusCode.BadRequest, ex);
      }

      return Request.CreateResponse(HttpStatusCode.BadRequest);
    }

  }
```

Now that we have created Token Controller, let us see how to validate it, when client passes token. Let us say, client has agreed to pass Token and API Key in the query string. Once the request comes, we will extract API key and Token from the query string and then get record for that token from the database. We will validate and make sure that token has not expired and is for the API Key passed.

*Code for Validating Token:*

```
public class ValidateTokenAttribute : AuthorizationFilterAttribute
  {
    [Inject]
    public CertificationsRepository TheRepository { get; set; }
    public override void OnAuthorization(HttpActionContext actionContext)
    {
      const string APIKEYNAME = "apikey";
      const string TOKENNAME = "token";

          var query = HttpUtility.ParseQueryString(actionContext.Request.RequestUri.Query);

      if (!string.IsNullOrWhiteSpace(query[APIKEYNAME]) &&
        !string.IsNullOrWhiteSpace(query[TOKENNAME]))
      {

        var apikey = query[APIKEYNAME];
        var token = query[TOKENNAME];

        var authToken = TheRepository.GetAuthToken(token);

            if (authToken != null && authToken.ApiUser.AppId == apikey &&
            authToken.Expiration > DateTime.UtcNow)
        {
          return;
```

```
                }
            else
                {
                    actionContext.Response =
                    actionContext.Request.CreateResponse(HttpStatusCode.Unauthorized);
                }
            }
        }
    }

}
```

## Same Origin Policy:

Same origin policy is a very important concept in browser security. It dictates that a web browser may only allow scripts on Page 1 to read data from Page 2, only if they have same origin (protocol, host and Port Number).

For example. Let us say you are logged into Facebook, and you visit a malicious website in another browser tab. Without same origin policy, this malicious website can read, post from your website account. However, with same origin policy, browser will not let this malicious site post on your Facebook account. But, what, if you want your API to be consumed from other domains. Let us see how we can overcome this limitation.

## CORS:

If you want that your API can be called from outside of your domain, then there are two ways to achieve it. One is using "JSONP" and other is by enabling CORS (Cross Origin Resource Sharing). In this exercise, we are going to focus on CORS.

To enable CORS in your project, you need to add "Microsoft.AspNet.WebApi.Cors" package in your project. Go to Tools-->NuGet Package Manager-->Manage NuGet Packages for Solution. Then go on the Browse tab and search for "CORS".

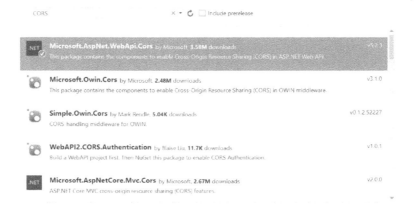

Install the "Microsoft.AspNet.WebApi.Cors" package. After that open WebApiConfig.cs file and add the following line of code in the Resister method.

Code: config.EnableCors();

To enable CORS at the controller level add "EnableCors("*","*","*") at the controller level:

*Sample Code for enabling CORS:*
```
[EnableCors("*","*","*")]
public class UsersController : BaseApiController
    {
        public UsersController(ICertificationRespository repo, IGetCurrentUserIdentity
getCurrentUserIdentityService) : base(repo)
        {

        }
```

To disable CORS at the Controller level add "DisableCors()" at the controller level.

Sample Code:

```
[DisableCors()]
    public class UsersController : BaseApiController
    {
        public UsersController(ICertificationRespository repo, IGetCurrentUserIdentity
            getCurrentUserIdentityService) : base(repo)
        {

        }
```

You can also override the setting at each method level. For example in the code below, I am enabling the CORS at the controller level but disabling it for Get Request.

Setting CORS at method level:

```
[EnableCors("*","*","*")]
    public class UsersController : BaseApiController
    {
        public UsersController(ICertificationRespository repo, IGetCurrentUserIdentity
                getCurrentUserIdentityService) : base(repo)
        {
        }

        [DisableCors]
        public IHttpActionResult Get()
        {
```

```
        return Ok(TheRepository.GetAllUsers().ToList().Select(x =>
        TheModelFactory.CreateUser(x)).ToList());


    }
```

## HTTPS:

If we want to force users to use HTTPS while making a request to Web API, then we need to create an attribute that inherits from "AuthorizationFilterAttribute" class and overrides "OnAuthorization" method. In this method, we will check if the request is "Get" or some other operation. If the request is "Get" then we will tell user that request is found, however they need to make this request using Https.

On the other hand, if request is Post, Put or delete we will return "NotFound".

*Code for forcing HTTPS:*

```
public class RequiredHttpsAttribute:AuthorizationFilterAttribute
    {
        public override void OnAuthorization(HttpActionContext actionContext)
        {
            var req = actionContext.Request;

            if (req.RequestUri.Scheme != Uri.UriSchemeHttps)
            {
                var html = "<p>Https is required.</p>";
                if (req.Method.Method == "GET")
                {
                    actionContext.Response = req.CreateResponse(HttpStatusCode.Found);
                    actionContext.Response.Content = new StringContent(html,
                    Encoding.UTF8, "text/html");

                    var uriBuilder = new UriBuilder(req.RequestUri);
                    uriBuilder.Scheme = Uri.UriSchemeHttps;
                    uriBuilder.Port = 443;

                    actionContext.Response.Headers.Location = uriBuilder.Uri;
                }
                else
                {
                    actionContext.Response = req.CreateResponse(HttpStatusCode.NotFound);
                    actionContext.Response.Content = new StringContent(html,
                    Encoding.UTF8, "text/html");
                }
            }
        }

    }
```

## Versioning:

When you create a new version of your Web API, you need to make sure that clients that are using old version of your API can continue to use it. There are number of ways to handle versioning in Web API. Let us look at couple of them.

1. One simple way to handle versioning is to create a new controller, add route for this controller. For Example: if your first version route is /API/Certificates then for your next version you can create a new controller say "CertificatesV1" and add route. Therefore, clients who want to use new version of API can use /API/CertificatesV1 as route. This is easy to implement but it is not a neat way to do it.
2. Another way of handling version is to ask client to pass version number they want to use either in the Header, or in the query string. For example client can make a request like this: /API/Certificates/10?v=2. What we will do is write our own controller selector, read the version number from query string or header and select controller accordingly.

*Code for Implementing Controller Selector:*

```
public class ControllerSelector : DefaultHttpControllerSelector
{
    private HttpConfiguration _config;
    public ControllerSelector(HttpConfiguration config)
    : base(config)
    {
        _config = config;
    }

    public override HttpControllerDescriptor SelectController
                                        (HttpRequestMessage request)
    {
        var controllers = GetControllerMapping();

        var routeData = request.GetRouteData();

        var controllerName = (string)routeData.Values["controller"];

        HttpControllerDescriptor descriptor;

        if (string.IsNullOrWhiteSpace(controllerName))
        {
            return base.SelectController(request);
        }
        else if (controllers.TryGetValue(controllerName, out descriptor))
        {
            var version = GetVersionFromQueryString(request);
            //var version = GetVersionFromHeader(request);
```

```csharp
            var newName = string.Concat(controllerName, "V", version);

            HttpControllerDescriptor versionedDescriptor;

            if (controllers.TryGetValue(newName, out versionedDescriptor))
            {
                return versionedDescriptor;
            }

            return descriptor;
        }

        return null;
    }

    private string GetVersionFromHeader(HttpRequestMessage request)
    {
        const string HEADER_NAME = "Version";

        if (request.Headers.Contains(HEADER_NAME))
        {
            var header = request.Headers.GetValues(HEADER_NAME).FirstOrDefault();
            if (header != null)
            {
                return header;
            }
        }

        return "1";
    }

    private string GetVersionFromQueryString(HttpRequestMessage request)
    {
        var query = HttpUtility.ParseQueryString(request.RequestUri.Query);
        var version = query["V"];

        if (version != null)
        {
            return version;
        }

        return "1";
    }
}
```

# THANK YOU

That's all I wanted to cover in this book. Thank you for reading my book. If you have any questions or suggestions related to book, feel free to email me at cloudsimplifiedforyou@gmail.com.